Look and Play
Noisy Animals

by Jim Pipe

Aladdin/Watts
London · Sydney

bee

A **bee** buzzes.

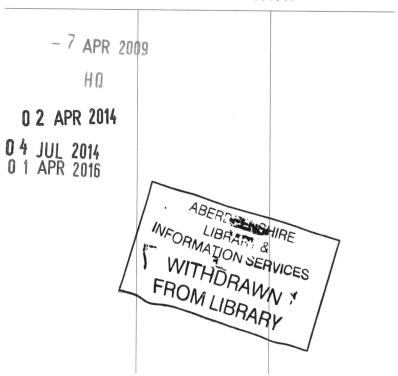
PIPE, Jim

Noisy animals

3

bat

4

A **bat** squeaks.

5

frog

A **frog** croaks.

7

snake

8

A **snake** hisses.

owl

An **owl** hoots.

gorilla

12

A **gorilla** grunts.

13

wolf

14

A **wolf** howls.

15

bear

16

A **bear** growls.

lion

18

A **lion** roars.

19

Who am I?

snake

bat

bear

frog

Match the words and pictures.

How many?

LET'S PLAY!

Can you count the noisy chicks?   21

What noise?

Squeak!

Hiss!

Roar!

Growl!

22   Can you sound like these animals?

Index

For Parents and Teachers

Questions you could ask:

p. 2 Can you sound like a bee? On each page encourage reader to make the animal's sound, and ask how it makes this sound, e.g. bee's wings make a buzzing sound, grasshopper's legs etc.

p. 4 What other animals squeak? e.g. mouse, rat. You could also explain that a bat's squeaks help it to find its way in the dark.

p. 6 How does a frog make a loud sound? By puffing up a big sack attached to its throat. Male frogs croak at night to attract females. The louder the croak, the further away females will hear them.

p. 10 When might you hear an owl? Owls are busy at night. Ask reader what other animal sounds they might hear at night, e.g. foxes, bats, crickets.

p. 12 Can you make a noise like a gorilla? Like us, gorillas make all sorts of noises: they roar, hoot, scream, cry, chuckle, hum, moan and burp! They also beat their hands on their chest.

p. 14 Why do wolves howl? Wolves howl to find other members of their family and to tell rivals to keep away. They often howl together like a choir!

p. 18 Do you think a lion makes a loud sound? Ask children to think of quiet and loud animals, e.g. mouse compared to elephant. However, lions need to be very quiet when they are hunting.

Activities you could do:

• Sing "Old Macdonald Had a Farm" but substitute "zoo" for farm and introduce a range of wild animals.

• Role play: encourage the reader to make noises using different parts of their body, e.g. stamping on ground like bull, noise of hooves by beating hands on a table, clapping hands like seal's flippers.

• Make nature sounds using simple instruments, e.g. make bullfrog sounds by twanging rubber band, make elephant sound using paper trumpet.

• Play a recording of animals' sounds, e.g. jungle noises. Ask children to shut their eyes and listen. Talk about what it must be like in the jungle.

© Aladdin Books Ltd 2007

Designed and produced by
Aladdin Books Ltd
2/3 Fitzroy Mews
London W1T 6DF

First published in 2007
in Great Britain
by Franklin Watts
338 Euston Road
London NW1 3BH

Franklin Watts Australia
Level 17/207 Kent Street
Sydney NSW 2000

Franklin Watts is a division of Hachette Children's Books.

ISBN 978 0 7496 7727 5

A catalogue record for this book is available from the British Library.

Dewey Classification: 590

Printed in Malaysia

Series consultant
Zoe Stillwell is an experienced Early Years teacher currently teaching at Pewley Down Infant School, Guildford.

Photocredits:
l-left, r-right, b-bottom, t-top, c-centre, m-middle
All photos on cover and insides from istockphoto.com except: 21 — Stockbyte. 22bl, tr & br – Corbis. 23mlb, tr & br — Ingram.